Cube

by Jennifer Boothroyd

first step nonfiction

Lerner Publications Company · Minneapolis

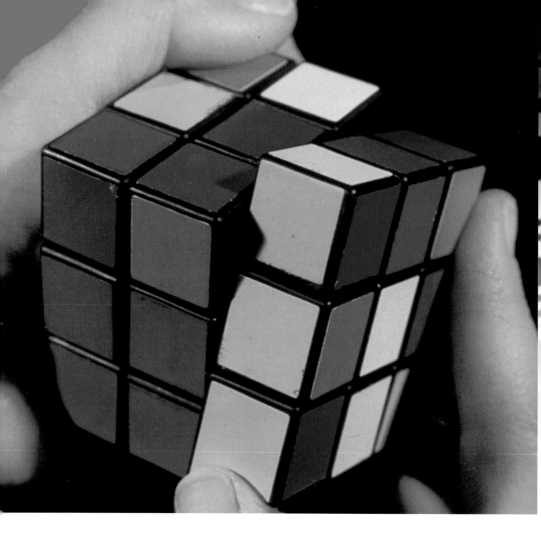

I see a cube.

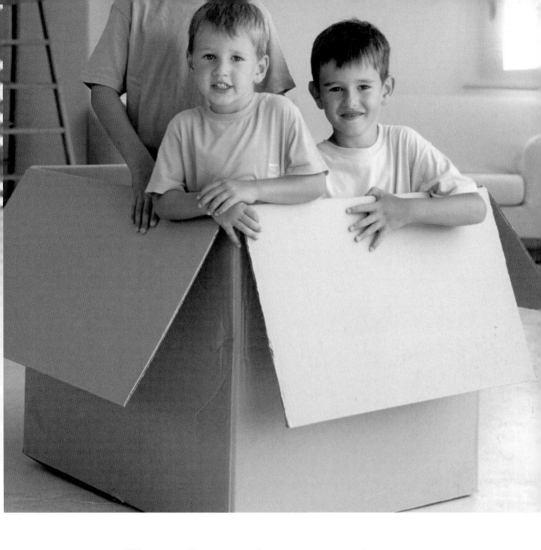

The box is a cube.

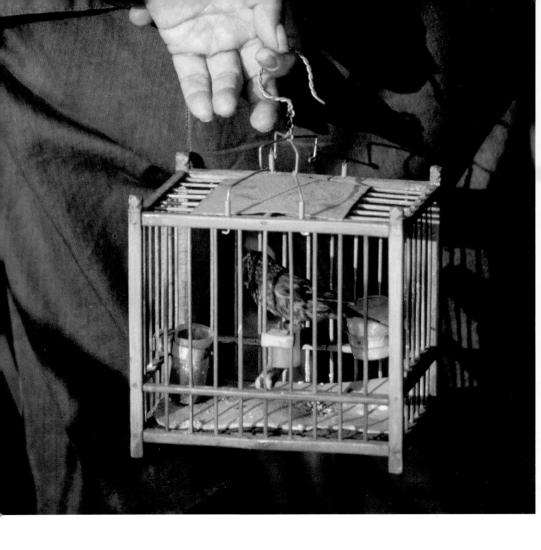

The cage is a cube.

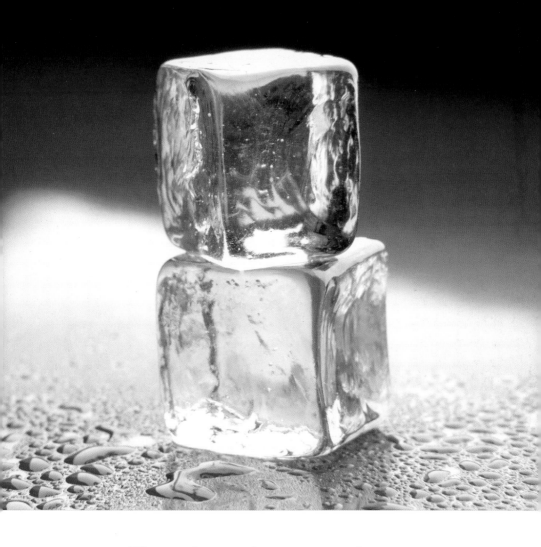

The ice is a cube.

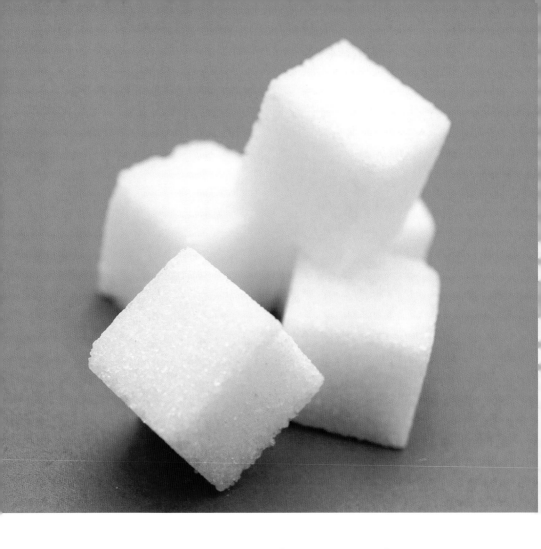

The sugar is a cube.

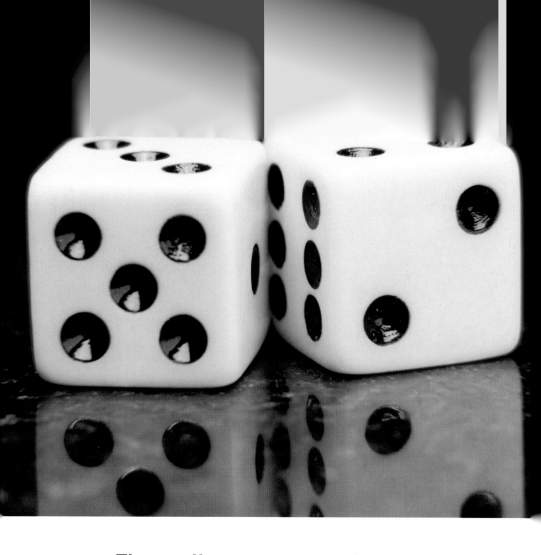

The dice are cubes.

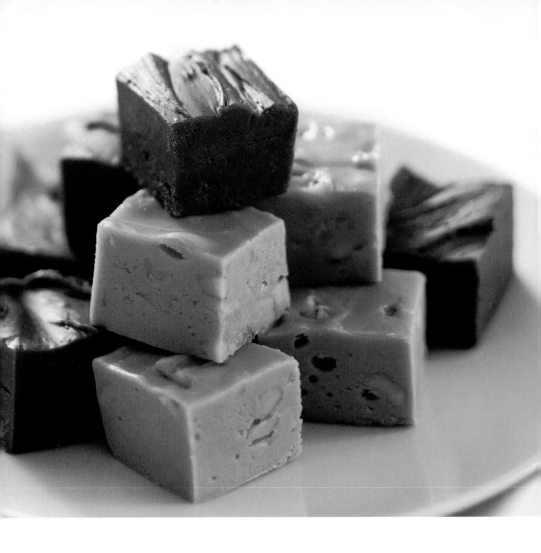

Do you see cubes?